Customer at the Core
A Practical Guide to Building Loyalty, Value, and Advocacy

BEYOND SATISFACTION

A Journey to Customer Centric Excellence

Dr. Saifuddin Kapasi

BlueRose ONE.com
Stories Matter
New Delhi • London

BLUEROSE PUBLISHERS
India | U.K.

For permissions requests or inquiries regarding this publication,
please contact:

BLUEROSE PUBLISHERS
www.BlueRoseONE.com
info@bluerosepublishers.com
+91 8882 898 898
+4407342408967

ISBN: 978-93-7310-704-2

Cover Design: Aman Sharma
Typesetting: Pooja Sharma

First Edition: September 2025

Dedication

To every customer who spoke up, every employee who listened, and every leader who chose long-term value over short-term convenience.

Acknowledgments

This book is the result of years of learning, teaching, unlearning, and listening. I would like to thank my colleagues, students, associates, and collaborators, your questions, ideas, and challenges have shaped this work in more ways than I can express.

To my team at Vodafone India Ltd, thank you for teaching me how customer centricity is practiced, not preached. To the clients I have had the privilege to guide as a Corporate Trainer, you showed me what excellence looks like in motion. And to every academic and professional mentor- thank you for pushing me towards clarity, rigor, and purpose.

Preface

In a world where customer expectations evolve faster than businesses can keep up, ***Beyond Satisfaction*** is a call to realign, rethink, and reimagine our deepest professional priorities.

My journey in Management Education has taught me the power of structured thinking, measurable frameworks, and academic rigor. But my conviction in customer-centric thinking truly deepened through *corporate practice*, notably during my tenure at **Vodafone India Ltd**, where I witnessed the power of experience-driven transformation. In my current role as a **Corporate Trainer and Business Coach**, I engage with organizations across industries including not for profit organisations to implement CXX strategies through hands-on learning, performance frameworks, and cultural alignment.

This book is my effort to integrate those worlds *boardroom pragmatism* and *academic depth* into a field guide for leaders, learners, and change-makers who want to matter to their customers, not just serve them.

Foreword by Arvind Agarwal

Everyone talks about customer centricity, but very few actually practice it by setting up processes to listen to the voice of the customer not as a choice, but as a rhythm. They measure scores from complaint to satisfaction to NPS and hold themselves accountable to the customer.

Having worked with great customer-centric organizations like Vodafone, Amazon, and Nykaa, I can totally relate to how organizations differ in their approach to customer centricity and what truly drives long-term success by going Beyond Satisfaction.

Dr. Saifuddin has articulated a very simple yet disciplined approach to customer centricity, based on his personal experiences at Vodafone and beyond. He is a practitioner himself, and his authenticity is self-evident throughout the book.

You don't need to be Jeff Bezos to understand these simple concepts and maximize long-term success through a customer-centric approach, one that manifests in compounding cash flow for truly customer-centric organizations like Amazon.

Arvind Agarwal is currently Group CFO PayU India

Prologue

Beyond Satisfaction – Why This Journey Matters Now

"Customers don't remember what you promised. They remember how you made them feel when it mattered most."

We live in a world where customer surveys are abundant, but customer trust is fragile. Where dashboards glow with metrics, but frontline teams still ask, "What do we do with this?" Where loyalty is chased through discounts, but rarely earned through dignity.

I have spent over three decades in boardrooms, classrooms, and shop floors. Have seen what happens when organizations treat customer experience as a department and what is possible when they treat it as a culture. Have seen metrics manipulated to look good on slides, seen a single act of empathy turn a detractor into a lifelong advocate.

This book was born from a simple but visionary realization:

Satisfaction is not enough.

Customers today want more than resolution. They want recognition.

They want to feel heard, not just helped.

They want to belong, not just buy.

Beyond Satisfaction is not a theory book. It is a field guide. A framework. A call to action. It is for leaders who are tired of chasing scores and ready to build systems of trust. It is for educators shaping the next generation of managers. And it is for every professional who believes that customer experience is not a metric but rather a mindset.

You will find tools here. Models. Templates. But more importantly, find a philosophy: that the most powerful business strategy is to care consistently, measurably, and meaningfully.

This is not a book about customer service.

It is a book about customer-centric leadership.

And it begins with one question:

"***What would happen if we designed every process, policy, and performance review with the customer's trust at heart***?"

Let's find out together.

Dr. Saifuddin Kapasi

Promoter Director, Educator, CX Advocate

Contents

PART I:
Foundations of Customer Centricity

Chapter 1: Why This Book, Why Now?

"Customers remember the experience longer than the product."

In today's hyper-informed and hyper-connected world, organizations are no longer just competing on price, product, or promotion, they are competing on **experience**.

And yet, despite the conversations around customer delight and service excellence, far too many businesses continue to confuse **satisfaction** with **loyalty**, **service delivery** with **strategic intimacy**, and **feedback** with **engagement**. What results is a shallow understanding of what customers truly value leading to churn, reputation loss, and missed opportunities.

This book was born out of those misalignments between **intention and execution**, and between what brands promise and what customers actually experience.

My own journey spanning **management education**, **corporate implementation at Vodafone India Ltd**, and **training engagements across industries** has shown me that what most teams need is not more theory, but a **field guide**. A structured, pragmatic roadmap that helps organizations redesign themselves around what matters most: the customer's trust and loyalty.

Whether you are a CXO, a frontline manager, a customer service head, a business developer, a faculty member, or a future leader, this book is for you. It will help you challenge assumptions, build robust systems, and develop a shared language around the evolving discipline of **Customer Centricity**.

Let's begin that journey - *beyond satisfaction.*

Chapter 2:
Defining Customer Centricity

"Customer Centricity is not a department. It's a discipline."

Chapter Objective

To define customer centricity as a business philosophy, cultural mindset, and operating model distinct from transactional service delivery or short-term customer satisfaction metrics.

In the realm of customer centricity, clarity of purpose is often clouded by vague gestures of goodwill. But as **Peter Fader aptly emphasizes,** *"Customer centricity is not about being customer-friendly. It's about identifying your most valuable customers and then doing everything you can to make them more valuable."* This perspective resonates with the structured approach to be driven, where centricity is not a slogan but a strategic commitment. The intentional idea being embed accountability, disciplined measurement, and empathy-driven execution, ensuring that customer-centricity is not merely aspirational but operational and cultural.

1. The Shift in Thinking

Business thinking has evolved through several eras:

- **Product-Centric:** "Build it well, and they will buy."
- **Sales-Centric:** "Sell it well, and we'll win the quarter."
- **Service-Centric:** "Respond well, and they'll stay satisfied."

The modern customer isn't looking to be served, they're looking to be *seen*. They expect **personalization**, **predictive assistance**, and a genuine **sense of partnership**.

2. Defining Customer Centricity

"Customer centricity is the intentional alignment of company culture, strategy, and operations to create sustained value *with* the customer, not just *for* the customer."

At the heart of Customer Centricity is **I.O.S.M**

- **Intentional:** It doesn't happen by chance, it's designed.
- **Organizational:** Everyone participates, not just service teams.
- **Sustainable:** Built for long-term relationships, not one-time interactions.
- **Mutual:** Value created must benefit both customer and enterprise.

3. Common Misconceptions

- **Myth 1:** "It's just good service."
- → No, centricity is a *design principle*, not a department.
- **Myth 2:** "It's a cost burden."
- → In truth, loyal customers reduce marketing spend and increase profitability.
- **Myth 3:** "It's only for B2C."
- → B2B ecosystems need it even more trust fuels multi-year decisions.

4. Traits of a Customer-Centric Organization

Trait	Description
Shared Understanding	Everyone knows the customer personas and goals
Feedback Loops	Listening and responding across channels
Experience Ownership	CX responsibilities are embedded across functions
Proactive Design	Experiences are predicted and curated
Metrics That Matter	NPS, retention, effort not just volume or value

5. Why It's Hard to Sustain

- **Siloed KPIs:** Teams optimize for their function, not the full journey
- **Short-Termism:** Quarterly targets override long-term loyalty
- **CX Governance Gaps:** No dedicated champions or accountability paths
- **Legacy Culture:** Fear of change, lack of measurement maturity

Quick Diagnostic: How Centric Are You?

- Are customers represented in strategic conversations?
- Are NPS or CX KPIs tied to incentives?
- Do employees feel empowered to deliver meaningful experiences?

If not, this book will help close those gaps.

Chapter 3:
Customer Centricity vs. Customer Satisfaction

"Satisfaction is a score. Centricity is a strategy."

1. Clarifying the Difference

Customer Satisfaction (CSAT):

Measures how customers feel about a specific service interaction, short-term, reactive.

Customer Centricity (CXX):

A long-term commitment to designing from the customer's lens, holistic, proactive.

2. The Limits of Satisfaction

Organizations often chase CSAT scores without realizing:

- High CSAT $\neq$ Loyalty
- "Satisfied" doesn't mean "Inspired" or "Engaged"
- Customers may rate an interaction highly even as they plan to switch

3. Why Centricity Outperforms Satisfaction

Satisfaction	Centricity
Reactive - "Was the service, okay?"	Proactive - "Are we meeting your evolving needs?"
Event-based evaluation	Journey-based transformation
Typically owned by Customer Service	Owned across functions
Easy to measure, hard to correlate	Requires effort but drives loyalty

4. What Happens When CSAT Becomes a Vanity Metric

Real-world example:

- A telco reported 88% CSAT scores, yet experienced 30% churn.
- Why? Customers were *satisfied* with resolution, but *disconnected* from the brand purpose and loyalty benefits.

5. Key Takeaways

- Satisfaction is a **moment**; centricity is a **movement**.
- CSAT is *one lens*, not the full picture.
- The new competitive advantage lies in deep emotional and experiential relevance not just problem-solving efficiency.

PART II:
Measuring What Matters

Chapter 4:
Customer Satisfaction Metrics and Their Limits

"What gets measured gets managed but only if you measure what matters."

Chapter Objective

To explore traditional customer satisfaction metrics, their practical applications, their limitations when used in isolation, and how to close the loop from satisfaction to loyalty.

1. The Usual Suspects: Common Metrics

1.1 CSAT (Customer Satisfaction Score)

CSAT asks customers to rate their satisfaction with a specific interaction, product, or service.

Calculation:

Count of positive responses (e.g., scores 4–5 on a 5-point scale).

1. Divided by total responses.
2. Multiplied by 100 to yield a percentage.

Use Cases:

- Post-support survey after a helpdesk ticket closes
- After onboarding or implementation milestones
- Quarterly check-ins on feature releases

Benefits:

- Diagnoses immediate pain points
- Easy for frontline teams to capture
- Benchmarks progress over time

Limitations:

- Transactional snapshot, not journey insight
- Scoring bias when teams incentivize "good" ratings
- Does not measure emotional loyalty

1.2 CES (Customer Effort Score)

CES gauges how much work a customer expended to achieve their goal.
Calculation: Average effort rating on a scale (e.g., 1 = Very Easy to 7 = Very Difficult).

Use Cases:

- Post-self-service portal interactions
- After complex processes like returns or membership upgrades
- Evaluating multi-step workflows in digital tools

Benefits:

- Correlates strongly with churn risk and advocacy
- Highlights friction points in processes
- Drives process-improvement initiatives

Limitations:

- Focuses on effort, not on satisfaction or delight
- Can miss emotional context (e.g., a difficult request that ends in a celebratory outcome)

2. Strengths of Satisfaction Metrics

- Quick to deploy and intuitive for both customers and teams
- Provide operational insights at transaction and touchpoint levels
- Tie directly to team performance goals and service SLAs

3. The Blind Spots

Strength	Limitation
Simple and direct	Lacks predictive power for long-term loyalty
Focused on discrete interactions	Ignores cumulative experience and emotional bonds
Easy to benchmark and compare	Vulnerable to manipulation (e.g., incentivized scoring)

4. Satisfaction Without Loyalty: A Dangerous Disconnect

A customer might score a support call a 5/5 after a speedy resolution, yet leave weeks later for a competitor with a more holistic experience. High CSAT can mask gaps in onboarding, product usability, or ongoing value. To bridge this gap, you need journey-level metrics like Net Promoter Score (NPS) and Customer Lifetime Value (CLV).

5. What to Watch For

- Include open-ended questions to capture nuance beyond numeric scores
- Track CSAT and CES alongside relationship metrics (e.g., NPS, CLV)
- Guard against complacency when satisfaction scores plateau

6. Beyond Satisfaction: Churn Rate and Retention

6.1 Churn Rate: Definition and Impact

Churn Rate = (Customers Lost ÷ Customers at Start of Period) × 100
High churn erodes recurring revenue and reverses acquisition gains, triggering costly root cause analyses and inter-departmental blame games.

6.2 Types of Churn

- Voluntary Churn: Customer actively cancels due to dissatisfaction or alternatives.
- Involuntary Churn: Lost due to payment failures, data issues, or fraud controls even when customers intend to stay.

6.3 Retention Rate: The Antidote

Retention Rate = (Customers at End of Period − New Customers) ÷ Customers at Start of Period × 100 Celebrates the combined efforts of sales and customer-facing teams to acquire, onboard, and continuously engage real customers.

7. Effective Strategies for Reducing Churn

7.1 Early Warning Indicators

- Monitor declining engagement (log-ins, feature usage)
- Track sentiment shifts in VoC data and social listening
- Flag increases in support tickets per account

7.2 Personalized Engagement

- Proactive check-ins by Customer Success Managers
- Tailored content or training for at-risk segments
- Dedicated executive sponsorship for high-value clients

7.3 Product and Service Enhancements

- Rapid response squads for urgent bugs or feature requests
- Continuous usability testing to eliminate friction
- Beta programs that let customers co-create new functions

7.4 Feedback Loops and Voice of Customer (VoC)

- Closed-loop follow-ups on every negative CES or CSAT
- Regular customer advisory councils to validate roadmap

- Internal dashboards combining survey, usage, and support data

8. Measuring and Improving Retention

8.1 Key Retention Metrics

- Renewal Rate: Percentage of customers who renew subscriptions
- Net Revenue Retention: Revenue retained from existing customers, including upsells and cross-sells
- Customer Health Score: Composite index (usage, satisfaction, sentiment)

8.2 Cohort Analysis

- Segment customers by acquisition date, plan, or industry
- Track each cohort's retention curve over time to spot anomalies
- Compare cohorts to test the impact of targeted interventions

8.3 Continuous Improvement Workflows

- Monthly churn-retention sprints with cross-functional teams
- A/B test retention offers and measure lift in renewal
- Root-cause dashboards that link churn events to product, pricing, or process issues

8.4 Ownership and Accountability

- Embed churn and retention goals into every department's KPIs
- Empower frontline reps with decision rights for small-scale win-backs
- Recognize and reward teams based on improvements in customer health scores

9. Integrating Metrics for a Holistic View

Combine moment-of-service metrics (CSAT, CES) with relationship indicators (NPS, CLV) and outcome measures (churn, retention). This triangulation pinpoints where to delight, simplify, or shore up loyalty before customers slip away.

Case Study:

Taming the Churn Tsunami: ABC Telecom's Retention Revolution

Background

ABC Telecom, a mid-sized regional mobile operator with 2.5 million subscribers, saw its monthly churn rate spike to 3.2% far above the industry benchmark. This churn wasn't just a number on a dashboard; it was eroding recurring revenue, straining acquisition budgets, and bruising the company's reputation.

The loss was coming from both voluntary churn (customers actively leaving) and involuntary churn (operator driven disconnections).

The leadership team took a decision and set up :

A VISON with A Mission

Disconnect to Reconnect: ABC Telecom's Churn Turnaround

And achieved

Echoes of Loyalty: Journey from Churn to Champion

Voluntary Churn – Customer Driven Exits through disconnection instructions

Customers cited:

- Price Pressure – Competitors' bundled data-voice-OTT packages undercut ABC's standalone tariffs.
- Service Quality Gaps – Persistent blackspots and call drops, particularly in rural-fringe areas.

- Billing Confusion – Surprise charges and complex invoices triggered "bill shock."
- Lifestyle Shifts – Increased adoption of Wi-Fi calling and OTT messaging apps reduced perceived need for mobile plans.
- Trust Erosion – Perception of overselling and poor transparency.

Involuntary Churn – Operator Driven suspension / disconnections of connections

ABC disconnected accounts due to:

- Non-payment and Credit Breaches - Missed bills and exceeded limits.
- Regulatory Non-Compliance - KYC lapses during onboarding.
- Fraud Controls - Blocking SIM box misuse.
- Dormant SIMs - Low-use accounts culled from the base.

Root Causes Identified

A churn task force found five interlinked issues:

1. Sales Overselling - New customers misled on tariff inclusions, discovering hidden costs later.
2. Coverage Weaknesses - Outages in fringe zones left gaps competitors exploited.
3. Roaming Surprises - High international roaming bills with no pre-travel notifications.
4. Inconsistent Support Quality - Outsourced and in-house agents delivered uneven service.
5. Siloed Leadership - Misaligned KPIs fostered a "not my problem" culture.

Discussion Questions

1. Which root cause should ABC address first for the fastest churn reduction?
2. How can sales incentives be redesigned to reward retention, not just sign-ups?
3. What billing transparency measures would prevent both domestic and roaming "bill shock"?
4. How can ABC unify training for outsourced and internal teams to ensure consistent customer experience?
5. What governance mechanisms could replace siloed KPIs with shared retention accountability?
6. Which early-warning metrics could help ABC spot churn risk before customers leave?

Solution Pathways

1. Sales Incentive Alignment

- Tie commissions to customer retention milestones (e.g., 6-month, 12-month mark). Have a effective commission Claw back policy which rewards genuine sales performance and penalises disguised performance.
- Use signed customer acknowledgements of plan features and limitations.
- Provide standardised product demos to avoid overpromising.

2. Network Reliability & Communication

- Deploy targeted coverage upgrades (e.g., small cells in blackspots).
- Send proactive outage alerts with restoration timelines.
- Publish quarterly "network scorecards" internally to motivate improvement.

3. Transparent Billing & Roaming

   - Centralise tariff and roaming rates on an easy-to-find "Clarity Hub."
   - Offer default daily roaming caps with opt-out flexibility.
   - Send post-travel cost summaries. Precede this with timely usage warning through effective alerts.

4. Consistent Customer Support

   - Establish a shared "Knowledge Academy" for all agents.
   - Maintain a single, updated knowledge base for products, tariffs, and troubleshooting.
   - Run regular mystery shopper calls to audit service standards.

5. Cross-Functional Leadership

   - Create a cross functional Retention Council with specific SMART Goals. Have Lead and Lag indicators drawn with weekly monitoring through review meets.
   - Align bonuses to churn reduction targets across Sales, CX, Network, and Finance.
   - Conduct quarterly churn retrospectives with action tracking.

Takeaway:

ABC Telecom's case shows that *high satisfaction scores in isolated touchpoints can't guarantee loyalty*. Without tackling underlying experience gaps, even delighted customers can churn. True retention demands coordinated fixes across sales honesty, network reliability, billing clarity, service consistency, and leadership alignment.

Chapter 5:
Decoding the Customer Experience (CXX)

"Customer Experience is how customers feel about what they remember."

Chapter Objective

To define Customer Experience (CXX), distinguish it from satisfaction, and outline how to map and measure it holistically.

1. What is CXX?

Customer Experience encompasses every interaction a customer has with a brand from marketing emails to in-store ambience to billing clarity.

It's how customers perceive your brand at every step, not just how they feel after a support call.

2. Mapping the Experience: Touchpoints and Emotions

- **Customer Journey Mapping**: A visual representation of every step in the customer lifecycle
- **Touchpoints**: Website visit, product use, support, delivery, feedback
- **Moments of Truth**: Critical interactions that make-or-break perception
- **Emotional Resonance**: How customers feel at each stage, not just what they do

3. Building a Journey Map

Stage	Touchpoint	Emotion	Opportunity
Awareness	Ad on Instagram	Curious	Personalize CTA
Purchase	Checkout process	Frustrated	Simplify interface
Post-purchase	Onboarding email	Reassured	Add community tips
Service	Live chat	Heard	Enable escalation easily

4. Tools for Experience Insights

- **Voice of Customer (VoC)**: Surveys, interviews, social listening
- **Customer Effort Score (CES)**: Especially for digital experiences
- **Empathy Mapping**: What customers think, feel, do, and speak

5. CXX vs CSAT in a Nutshell

CSAT	CXX
Measures a moment	Measures an entire journey
Output of service	Strategy across touchpoints
Mostly reactive	Anticipatory and proactive

Chapter 6:
Net Promoter Score (NPS) – What, Why, and How

"The one number you need to grow."

Fred Reichheld, creator of NPS

Chapter Objective

To introduce Net Promoter Score (NPS), explain its logic and value, and outline how it connects to customer centricity excellence.

1. What is NPS?

A simple yet powerful loyalty metric based on one question:

"On a scale of 0–10, how likely are you to recommend our products or services to a friend or colleague?"

Customers are categorized into:

- **Promoters (9–10)**: Loyal, enthusiastic, value drivers
- **Passives (7–8)**: Satisfied but vulnerable to churn
- **Detractors (0–6)**: Disappointed or frustrated, may damage brand

NPS = % Promoters – % Detractors [Passives are not counted]

2. Why It Works

- Links directly to loyalty and advocacy
- Easy to benchmark across industries
- Can be asked post-transaction or on a relationship basis
- Drives **closing the loop**: following up with unhappy customers

1. **My Experience: NPS in Practice**

During my time at Vodafone, we didn't just track NPS as a metric, we embedded it into the culture. Every score was an invitation to listen deeper. We conducted NPS reviews to diagnose experience gaps across functions and service line, and we built CX rituals around those learnings.

This was not just confined to conference rooms. We practiced **Gemba** - the art of going to the right place where value is created. Our teams visited **partner call centres**, **field agencies**, and **our stores**, not as auditors but as learners. We listened not only to customers but to the frontline teams who shaped those experiences hour by hour. We saw real interactions. We heard frustration, and we heard hope.

We encouraged **constructive listening,** not defensiveness, not denial. Detractor feedback was treated with respect, not resistance. And we went a step further:

We **celebrated problems**.

Yes, celebrated.

Because every complaint carried the seed of a reform. We recognized and rewarded those who surfaced issues, even before they became visible in reports. It wasn't just about closing loops, it was about **opening eyes**.

CX insights weren't siloed in a strategy department. We democratized them. We gave ownership to the teams who could act, whether it was a billing associate, a customer service supervisor, or a field technician. And we saw firsthand how that empowerment turned passive metrics into passionate reform.

Our NPS journey wasn't about chasing numbers. It was about chasing meaning. And the deeper we listened, the clearer it became: the voice of the customer isn't just data it's **direction**.

- Our **passive-to-promoter conversion increased**
- We rolled out **targeted onboarding content** for customers across various functions and we aligned processes in Credit & Collections to believe in Customer First.
- Contact centre training included **NPS emotion mapping** to increase empathy specially in functions like Collections where agents became enablers for payment rather than mere collection agents

NPS transformed from a score into a **system of cultural accountability**.

4. Closing the Loop

NPS only creates value when:

- Feedback is acted upon (especially detractor comments)
- Root cause is investigated and fixed
- Promoters are celebrated and retained
- Employees receive transparent visibility into scores

Chapter 7: Closing the Loop with Purpose - NPS Actions That Drive Change

Chapter Objective

To guide organizations in translating Net Promoter Score (NPS) insights into structured, cross-functional action by cascading feedback, going to the Gemba, and applying Lean principles to improve customer experience.

1. The Power of the Score Lies in What You Do After

Collecting NPS is not the goal, it's the beginning.

High-performing teams treat the score as a **trigger for alignment**, not just a result to be celebrated or feared. The magic lies in:

- **Closing the loop** with customers
- **Opening conversations** between teams
- **Sustaining momentum** through process ownership

"The score is the symptom. The comment is the clue. The action is the cure."

2. Cascade, Discuss, Align

The first step after any NPS cycle is to **activate the organization**. Here's how:

- **Start with the leadership team**: Present NPS by segment, geography, product, and function
- **Cascade insights cross-functionally** to CX, Ops, Sales, HR, Product teams

- Hold **focused discussions on the 'why' behind scores**, not just the numbers
- **Separate Promoters, Passives, and Detractors** - analysing themes, emotional cues, and business risks

CX debriefs must shift from passive score reviews to **active recovery and insight-led sprints**.

3. Go to the Gemba – Where Experience Actually Happens

"Gemba" is the real place, the frontline where customer value is created and destroyed.

What Is Gemba in CX?

- The **help desk call** where a complaint is either resolved or escalated
- The **delivery doorstep** where a promise is fulfilled or broken
- The **app interface** where a loyal user either feels understood or lost

Gemba is not the boardroom. It's the moment where **emotion meets execution**.

Why It Matters

- It builds **empathy** between teams and customers
- Shows **real-world friction**, beyond dashboards
- Inspires **grassroots solutions** that are often missed by leadership
- Bridges silos - frontline employees become teachers, not just executors

How to Practice Gemba-Based CX

- **Shadow your teams**: Watch live interactions, record observations, avoid interference

- Run **CX Observation Sprints**: Map customer steps and employee reactions
- Launch **Listening Logs**: Encourage staff to submit stories and breakdowns weekly
- Create **"Walk & Talk" CX rituals**: Managers spend time at call centres, branches, kitchens, etc.

"Gemba isn't inspection. It's immersion."

4. Diagnose Muda, Mura, Muri in Customer Journeys

Adapted from Lean practice, these three forms of inefficiency are everywhere in CX.

Concept	Meaning	CX Application
Muda	Waste	Repetitive questions, multiple calls, redundant steps
Mura	Unevenness	Inconsistent service levels, unpredictable wait times
Muri	Overburden	Fatigued systems, rushed staff, unrealistic expectations

Why Use These Principles?

- They uncover **hidden cost to customer effort**
- Shift CX from "soft" perception to **process discipline**
- Help teams eliminate what frustrates customers *and* employees alike

How to Diagnose Effectively

- Use **Color-Coded CX Cards**: Teams tag moments as Muda (red), Mura (yellow), Muri (blue)
- Create **Frontline Forums**: Staff identify where burden or waste slows them down

- Analyse **NPS verbatims**: Look for phrases like "too slow," "always different," "I was exhausted"

Design interventions based on these tags - simplify, standardize, empower.

5. Benefits of Doing It This Way

- **Higher NPS through smoother journeys**
- **Faster root cause identification**
- **Greater team buy-in and morale**
- **Reduction in churn, complaints, and effort scores**
- **Leadership credibility as doers, not just reviewers**

"When we fix what customers feel, and not just what leaders assume, transformation begins."

Closing Checklist – NPS Action Cadence

Step	Owner
Score Cascade to Management Teams	CX Lead / CEO
Segment-wise Debrief	Marketing / Ops / Product
Gemba Sprint Scheduled	CX Council
Muda–Mura–Muri Tagging Session	Frontline Team Leads
Quick Win Tracker Activation	Improvement Champion
Follow-up to Customers	Service / CRM Teams

Final Takeaway

NPS is not just feedback. It's the **beginning of accountability**.

Organizations that cascade data, walk the floor, and design recovery from the customer's lens earn something metrics can't buy: **trust, loyalty, and internal pride**.

"What matters is not what the score says, but what your teams do next."

Chapter 8:
Using NPS for Growth – Surveys, Insights, and Action

"Don't ask what your score is. Ask what your score is telling you."

Chapter Objective

To help readers design NPS systems that lead to actionable, measurable improvements across the organization.

1. Setting Up Your NPS System

- **Transaction vs Relationship NPS**
- Transactional = after purchase or service
- Relationship = periodically, to assess brand sentiment
- **Design Tips**
- Keep the core question unchanged, but add:
- "What is the primary reason for your score?"
- "What could we do to improve?"

2. Common NPS Pitfalls

- Treating it as a vanity metric ("We hit 45 NPS!")
- Lack of contextual analysis by segment or channel
- Not personalizing follow-up for detractors
- Ignoring **passives**, who are quiet churn risks

3. NPS Dashboard Snapshot (from earlier)

Metric	Purpose
Overall NPS	CX health score
Segment NPS	Insights by product line or demographic
Channel NPS	Performance of app, web, in-store, etc.
Closed-Loop Feedback %	Follow-through on detractor alerts
NPS-Linked KPAs	Aligning CX with team performance reviews

4. Connecting NPS to Organizational Growth

- NPS-positive segments tend to renew, refer, and buy more
- Helps identify CX heroes internally
- Promoters can co-create innovation and advocacy campaigns
- Sustained NPS improvements can influence **stock performance**, **brand valuation**, and **employee morale**

Chapter 9:
From Score to Shopfloor - Root Cause, Rhythm, and Reform

Chapter Objective

To help organizations move beyond insight generation to experience-led reform using structured action cycles, sprint planning, and cross-functional accountability to raise NPS through real-world changes.

1. The Limitations of Reflection Without Rhythm

Many organizations get stuck between "knowing" and "doing." After CX review meetings:

- Reports are saved but not shared
- Teams nod in agreement but defer action
- Momentum stalls until the next NPS cycle

The missing element? **Execution rhythm.**

What you need is a repeatable system that moves insights into reform with clarity, cadence, and accountability.

"A good CX system doesn't just highlight gaps, it mobilizes teams to close them."

2. The Sprint Mindset – Quick Wins with Lasting Impact

Apply Agile principles to CX reform:

Sprint Definition

A short, time-bound initiative focused on one CX gap co-owned by cross-functional team members.

CX Sprint Ingredients

Component	Description
Focus Area	One NPS theme, moment, or issue
Team	4–6 members from relevant departments
Duration	2–3 weeks
Output	Fix deployed + feedback captured
Review Mechanism	Sprint retrospective shared org-wide

Examples

- Redesigning a confusing payment page
- Training delivery staff on post-drop empathy scripts
- Resolving delay patterns flagged in Muri diagnostics

3. Experience Labs – Co-Creating Better Journeys

CX Labs are informal yet structured spaces where ideas, issues, and innovations are surfaced collaboratively.

Element	Purpose
CX Narratives	Share Promoter and Detractor stories
Journey Review Boards	Map points of friction and resolution
Innovation Wall	Employee-sourced ideas for CX improvements
Test & Deploy Station	Trial small changes before organization-wide

"Labs turn listening into learning and learning into launching."

Encourage even junior employees to submit stories or ideas. Ownership builds advocacy.

4. Reform Tracker – CX Governance in Motion

Track every action from insight to implementation:

Tracker Field	Description
NPS Gap/Theme	Area identified for action
Sprint Owner	Responsible CX champion
Root Cause	Summary of customer feedback + internal audit
Action Taken	What was changed, updated, simplified
Impact Review Date	When and how results will be measured

This creates traceability, transparency, and **continuous improvement culture**.

5. Empowering the Right Roles

CX reform doesn't belong only to CX teams. It thrives when embedded:

- **Product** owners redesign flows based on friction themes
- **Tech** engineers simplify interfaces in response to Muda flags
- **HR** embeds CX actions into onboarding and recognition
- **Finance** aligns billing clarity with sentiment triggers
- **Service** leaders use complaint trends for empathy coaching

Everyone has a CX role. Make it visible and measurable.

Final Takeaway

Insight alone isn't enough.

You must build rhythms of **response, reform, and reactivation.**

"Customers don't reward what we know, they reward what we change."

Let your CX journey not just be strategic but sprint ready, story-driven, and people powered.

PART III:
Building a Customer-Centric Organization

Chapter 10:
Aligning Structure to Experience – Roles & Rewards

"What gets rewarded gets repeated." - *Michael LeBoeuf*

Chapter Objective

To explore how organizational design, people practices, and incentives must evolve to support a truly customer-centric enterprise.

1. Making Centricity Everyone's Job

Customer experience is not just the job of a CX team or a call centre, it's a shared responsibility. True centric organizations:

- Define CX roles and KPAs across departments
- Empower employees to solve customer problems directly
- Align structure with accountability

2. HR as a CX Architect

HR plays a critical role in bringing centricity to life by:

- **Hiring for empathy and ownership**
- **Integrating CX into job descriptions and performance reviews**
- **Recognizing behaviours that support long-term customer value**

You don't just recruit for skills, you recruit for *alignment*.

3. Redesigning Rewards Systems

Organizations must evolve from rewarding only efficiency and volume to **recognizing impact on customer outcomes**. Examples:

Traditional Metric	CX-Enhanced Metric
Calls handled per hour	% of issues resolved without escalation
Sales closed	NPS of referred clients
Time-to-resolution	First contact resolution AND customer sentiment

Introduce **CX Champions Awards**, tie bonuses to **team NPS shifts**, and celebrate employees recognized in VoC feedback.

4. Real Example: NPS-Linked Recognition in Action

At one of our partner BPO organizations, performance appraisals included:

- NPS feedback from each agent's serviced customer pool
- Peer feedback on collaboration in closing complaints
- Monthly CX Hero features in internal newsletters

Result? Employee engagement rose, and churn dropped by 11%.

5. Build it into Org Charts

- Assign CX leads in every vertical, not just marketing
- Ensure the CX Office collaborates with HR, IT, ops, finance
- Cross-functional working groups for CX problem-solving

Customer centricity must be visible *on paper,* not just in slogans.

Chapter 11:
Creating Advocates Inside and Out

"Engaged employees create loyal customers. Loyal customers drive sustainable growth."

Chapter Objective

To show how internal culture, values, rituals and storytelling create customer impact

1. The Mirror Effect: EX = CX

If employees feel empowered, included, and proud they will reflect that in every customer touchpoint. What lives inside, shows outside.

2. Activate Internal Champions

- Appoint "CX Stewards" in every team to collect and share customer stories
- Equip frontline staff with tools, training, and time to delight
- Run CX Week, Customer Voice Days, internal "empathy challenges"

3. Make Culture Tangible

- Embed customer stories in town halls, newsletters, onboarding
- Frame customer impact alongside business KPIs
- Invite Promoters and Detractors to internal storytelling sessions

4. Staff Listening Systems

- Internal NPS: How likely are employees to recommend the company to customers?
- Experience Cafés: Cross-functional feedback sessions

- Exit interviews focused on CX gaps

5. Case Insight: Building Internal Advocacy in a Startup

A mid-size Indian fintech startup created a cross-team ritual called **"Voice of the Week"**, where one promoter or detractor story was shared and discussed. It created empathy, clarity, and sparked three major UX improvements, all led by non-CX teams.

Chapter 12:
Empathy in Action

Emotional Experience as a Loyalty Engine

Chapter Objective

To explore how emotional resonance, authentic empathy, and structured complaint engagement shape customer loyalty and how organizations can embed these into daily CX practices, training, and performance systems.

1. Emotional Value: The Missing Differentiator

Most brands compete on price, speed, or convenience. Few focus on what customers feel.

And yet, emotionally connected customers:

- Spend more
- Stay longer
- Promote more
- Forgive more when things go wrong

They become advocates, not just consumers. Why? Because the brand has earned their trust through emotion.

"In the age of AI and automation, emotion is the last mile of connection."

2. Decoding Emotional Loyalty

Customer loyalty can be transactional ("I get points") or habitual ("It's convenient"). Emotional loyalty, however, arises from:

- Empathic interactions
- Shared values

- Memorable recovery moments
- Consistent dignity in service

Type of Loyalty	Trigger	Stability
Transactional	Discounts, points	Fragile
Functional	Convenience, ease	Moderate
Emotional	Care, connection, empathy	Resilient

3. Empathy – Not a Trait, But a Training

Empathy isn't just personality, it's process. And yes, it can be trained.

EMPACT Framework for Empathy-Driven CX

Element	Practice Example
E – Engage	Look up from the screen. Make human contact.
M – Mirror	Reflect what they're feeling: "That sounds frustrating."
P – Personalize	Use their name, context, and history, not a script.
A – Anticipate	Proactively address needs before asked.
C – Care	Stay calm, present, and genuinely invested.
T – Thank	Close with gratitude, not just resolution.

Train teams to use EMPACT across touchpoints, calls, chats, in-store moments, complaints.

4. Designing Experiences with Empathy

Empathy is best embedded through micro-choices across journeys. Ask:

- *"Is this process easy and affirming?"*
- *"Does our language convey dignity?"*

- *"Are our policies flexible when customers are vulnerable?"*

Examples:

Touchpoint	Empathic Signal
Billing dispute	"We understand this is stressful, let's walk through it."
Missed delivery	"Here's how we'll make it easier next time."
Support escalation	"You shouldn't have had to wait, thank you for your patience."

5. Loyalty Through Retention Rituals

Retention is not about bribes, it's about rituals of care and continuity.

Smart Retention Programs

- Milestone Moments: Personal messages on anniversaries or birthdays
- Recovery Thank-Yous: Appreciation after issue resolution
- Feedback Loops: Show what changed based on customer input
- Co-Creation Labs: Invite customers into product testing and advisory roles

Retention lives in stories, not spreadsheets.

6. Celebrate Complaints – Elevate Learning

Complaints are not threats, they are gifts of truth.

Treat complaints as:

- Unfiltered market intelligence
- Coaching material for empathy training
- Signals of trust (if they didn't care, they wouldn't complain)

Build a Complaint Wisdom System

Component	Purpose
Complaint Data Bank	Archive issue types, emotions, and outcomes
Recovery Ritual Templates	Structured response playbooks with empathy focus
Learning Library	Use real cases in onboarding and CX workshops
CX Hero Recognition	Spotlight staff who transform pain into loyalty

"The loudest complaint is sometimes a love letter masked in frustration."

7. Measuring Emotional Impact

Go beyond resolution rates. Measure *how customers felt* and *how deeply they reconnected.*

Tools to Use:

- Empathy KPIs: % of customers who felt heard and valued
- Sentiment Analysis: AI or manual tagging of emotional tone
- Recovery NPS: Track NPS uplift after complaint resolution
- Voice of Heart Surveys: "Do you feel you belong with us?"

Final Takeaway

Empathy is the strongest currency in customer relationships.

It doesn't cost extra but its returns are exponential.

"The most memorable experiences aren't perfect, they're the ones where imperfection met humanity."

Let loyalty be shaped not by discounts but by dignity.

Chapter 13:
CX Governance & Maturity Models

"Without structure, centricity is a conversation. With governance, it becomes a capability."

Chapter Objective

To establish the need for CX governance models and show how maturity ladders guide experience evolution.

1. What is CX Governance?

A system of accountability, cadence, cross-functional ownership, and metrics that ensures customer experience is measured, discussed, and improved *intentionally*.

2. Components of Good CX Governance

- **CX Council**: Leaders from CX, Ops, HR, Marketing, Product
- **Experience Scorecard**: NPS, CES, complaint resolution metrics
- **Monthly Reviews**: Customer stories, risks, closures
- **Annual Charter**: CX strategy integrated into business roadmap

3. The ACE Framework

Element	Action
Alignment	CX KPIs aligned with strategic priorities
Consistency	Harmonized experiences across touchpoints
Empathy	Culture and training investments in deep customer care

4. CX Maturity Ladder

Level	Stage	Traits
Level 1	Reactive	Firefighting complaints, no CX strategy
Level 2	Basic Feedback	Simple surveys, limited insights
Level 3	Managed CX	VoC system + NPS used, ad-hoc improvements
Level 4	Cross-Functional CX	CX KPIs tied to roles, quarterly reviews
Level 5	Predictive and Adaptive	AI, personalization, experience design is proactive

5. Case Study: A Manufacturer's Leap from Level 2 to 4

A mid-sized home appliances company went from basic CSAT to full NPS integration in 12 months. How?

- Created a CX Lead role and a NPS council and rolled out NPS journey. Published NPS scores and took action at NPS council on areas to improve which would essentially improve Promoters, move passives to promoters and remedy issues which lead to Detractors.
- Launched quarterly VoC reviews with ops, logistics, support
- Linked warehouse accuracy to regional NPS
- Trained delivery agents on empathy and post-delivery follow-ups

They didn't just raise scores, they rebuilt reputation and referrals.

PART IV:
The Road Ahead

Chapter 14:
Complaint Wisdom

Turning Pain in to Progress – Building a Loyalty Data Bank

Chapter Objective

To reframe customer complaints from risk into resource, transforming them into structured insight, empathy training, and CX innovation through a robust internal learning system.

1. Why Complaints Deserve Celebration

Organizations often treat complaints as exceptions, anomalies to fix and forget.

But in truth, complaints are:

- **Signals of unmet expectations**
- **Evidence of care** - customers who no longer care, don't bother complaining
- **Loyalty inflection points** - how a complaint is handled determines future advocacy

"Every complaint is a gift wrapped in frustration, waiting to be unboxed with humility."

Great CX cultures celebrate complaints. Not because they happened but because they teach.

2. Complaint vs. Feedback – Understand the Nuance

Aspect	Complaint	Feedback
Intent	Expressing dissatisfaction or pain	Offering suggestions or reflections
Emotional tone	Often urgent, frustrated, emotional	Neutral, constructive, informational
Opportunity	Fix what broke, heal what hurt	Improve what works or innovate further
Response urgency	Immediate, personalized, visible closure	Considered, systemic input

Both matter but complaints offer **raw honesty under pressure**.

3. The Loyalty Potential Hidden in Complaints

Handling a complaint with empathy and speed leads to:

- **Recovered trust**
- **Improved NPS among Detractors**
- **Emotional stickiness** - "They actually cared about fixing it"
- **Referrals** based on recovery story, not just product satisfaction

Studies show that customers who had a problem *and* saw it resolved well are often more loyal than those who had no problem at all.

4. Building a Loyalty Data Bank – Components & Functions

Create an internal system that captures, learns from, and reuses complaint insights across departments.

Core Components

Element	Function
Complaint Categorizer	Tags by type, touchpoint, tone, resolution speed
Emotion Tracker	Logs customer sentiment (anger, confusion, sadness)
Root Cause Mapper	Links complaint themes to Muda–Mura–Muri flags
Action Tracker	Shows what reform occurred, who led it, and NPS impact
CX Wisdom Wall	Curates resolved complaint stories for training
Playback Library	Stores anonymized voice/chat transcripts for empathy workshops

5. Creating a Culture That Welcomes Complaints

Steps to Shift Mindset:

- Train teams to say: *"Thank you for bringing this to us."*
- Celebrate internal *Complaint Champions* staff who turn complaints into "Thank You" moments
- Integrate complaint wisdom into **town halls, newsletters, onboarding decks**
- Create a **"Voice of Disappointment" playback series** used in training and process reform labs

"Complaints show the gap between our intentions and their perceptions. Closing that gap is growth."

6. How to Use Complaints in CX Training

Complaints are emotionally rich. Use them to:

- Teach **empathy through real-world breakdowns**
- Develop **recovery playbooks** with context and dignity

- Role-play scenarios drawn from actual cases
- Hold **quarterly "Complaint Clinics"** where teams analyse, debate, and redesign problem zones

Use anonymized transcripts or simulated scenarios to practice response tone, escalation, and empathy cadence.

7. Measuring the Impact of Complaint Wisdom

Track how well your organization learns from its pain points.

Metric	What It Tells You
Recovery NPS (Post-Resolution)	Loyalty impact of your service recovery style
Complaint-to-Reform Ratio	% of complaints that led to tangible changes
Resolution Empathy Index	Feedback on tone and human handling
Repeat Complaint Rate	Shows effectiveness of long-term fixes
CX Training Embedding Rate	% of training content sourced from real cases

These metrics turn complaint handling into a **strategic growth pathway**, not just damage control.

Final Takeaway

"The fastest way to customer loyalty is through recovery. The fastest way to recovery is through empathy. The fastest path to empathy is complaint wisdom."

Don't fear complaints. Invite them. Investigate them. And teach from them.

Because every time a customer tells you where it hurt, they're also giving you a chance to **heal the brand and deepen the bond**.

Chapter 15:
Customer Trust in the Digital World

"If experience is the product, trust is the packaging."

Chapter Objective

To explore the evolving relationship between data, transparency, and customer loyalty in an increasingly digital, automated world.

1. Why Trust Is Now Strategy

- Customers exchange **data for value** but only when they feel in control.
- The rise of AI and personalization has made trust a **design requirement**.
- Transparency, responsiveness, and **consent-driven CX** are non-negotiables.

2. Pillars of Digital Trust

Pillar	Description
Transparency	Clear data usage policies, cookie control, opt-ins
Integrity	Delivering on brand promises, even under pressure
Responsiveness	Quick resolution during breaches, recalls, or misinformation
Empathy	Designing interfaces and experiences with human dignity

3. Ethical Personalization

- Avoid creepy or manipulative nudges
- Provide meaningful opt-outs

- Let customers "train" their own experience (e.g., "Show me less of this")

4. Case Example: The Power of Recovery

A leading e-retailer experienced a delivery breach. Instead of burying the error:

- They proactively emailed all affected customers
- Gave a direct line to a service head
- Offered a transparent post-mortem

NPS among those affected was higher than the average segment a clear signal that **trust isn't about perfection. It's about honesty.**

Chapter 16:
CX Trends Shaping the Future

"The future of business is experiences made smarter, faster, and more human."

Chapter Objective

To spotlight the key trends defining experience design, measurement, and delivery in the coming years.

1. AI-Powered Hyper personalization

- AI curates in-the-moment experiences based on behaviour, history, and intent
- Use responsibly to add value, not overwhelm
- Predictive CX: Fixing issues before customers raise them

2. Omnichannel Is the New Default

- Channel-hopping is normal (app → store → WhatsApp)
- CX excellence = consistent identity and memory across all channels
- Tools: CRM overlays, unified ticketing, and preference-based engagement

3. Emotion Analytics and Sentiment Scoring

- Voice tone, word choice, facial cues inform frontline and AI agents
- Brands can respond in *emotionally intelligent ways*
- Tip: Pair sentiment scoring with human judgment to avoid bias traps

4. Immersive & Assisted Experiences

- Augmented Reality (AR): Try-on apps, interactive stores
- Virtual Reality (VR): Remote banking, property tours, learning modules
- Assisted CX: Smart assistants & co-browsing for real-time guidance

5. Experience-Led Business Strategy

- CX roles now report to the C-suite
- Metrics like NPS, customer retention, and digital satisfaction influence capital allocation
- Companies winning the CX game outpace revenue growth vs peers

Chapter 17:
The Centricity Playbook

Templates, diagnostics, and KPIs for embedding CX into your organization.

Chapter Objective

To provide a toolkit of templates, diagnostics, and prompts for readers to begin embedding customer centricity in their own organizations immediately.

1. CX Maturity Diagnostic

Rate your organization across five pillars (scale 1–5):

- Leadership commitment to CX
- Integration of CX KPIs in reviews
- Presence of a VoC system
- Feedback loops and action tracking
- CX training and onboarding for all teams

Total your score → Find your level on the CX Maturity Ladder (1–5)

Use this to define your Year 1 roadmap.

2. The Customer Experience Charter

A living document that outlines your company's:

- Experience philosophy
- Customer promises
- Listening and escalation mechanisms
- Governance and improvement routines
- Shared metrics and ownership

Co-create this with leaders, service teams, and even customers.

3. Journey Mapping Templates

Step	Touchpoints	Customer Emotion	Team Ownership	CX Goals
Product Research	Website, Ads	Curious	Marketing	Inspire & educate
Purchase	Cart, Payment	Anxious	Product + Tech	Reassure & simplify
Onboarding	Email, App	Hopeful	Success Team	Set Expectations
Support	Chat, Call Centre	Frustrated	Service Ops	Solve & recover

4. Experience KPAs by Function

Suggest measurable goals per team:

- **HR**: % employees trained on empathy and CX
- **Finance**: Billing NPS or delay resolution rate
- **Marketing**: Increase in promoter referrals
- **Logistics**: On-time delivery % + post-delivery rating
- **Technology**: App store ratings, page speed, downtime tracking

5. Tools Index for Implementation

Tool	Use Case
NPS Scorecard Template	Weekly/monthly tracking
CX Governance Framework	Structure and accountability
Experience KPI Sheet	Tie business metrics to CX outcomes
VoC Tracker	Feedback source logging and analysis
Centricity Maturity Ladder	Roadmap for evolution

Chapter 18:
NPS in Action – Adapting Across Industries

"If loyalty is the goal, NPS is the compass, no matter where you serve."

Chapter Objective

To showcase how Net Promoter Score (NPS) can be meaningfully applied and tailored across various industries ranging from hospitality to community services to education by outlining what it measures, why it matters, how it can be implemented, when to collect it, and what to take away.

Why This Chapter Matters

NPS is often viewed as a one-size-fits-all survey. In reality, its power lies in how it's **contextualized to the emotional and operational journeys** of different sectors. Whether you're flying a customer across continents, serving a family dinner, organizing a community pilgrimage, or guiding a student toward transformation - *experience matters*. And NPS helps you measure not just satisfaction, but **advocacy**.

Let's explore five key sectors where NPS can unlock powerful insights when implemented thoughtfully.

1. Travel, Hotel & Airline Industry

"People travel for the destination but return for the experience."

- **What:** NPS captures loyalty across pre-booking, journey quality, and post-stay memory.
- **Why:** Travel is emotionally charged; memories determine referrals.

- **How:** Deploy NPS post-flight, post-checkout, or app usage via SMS, app prompts, or email.
- **When:** 24–48 hours after experience for freshness and actionability.
- **Takeaways:**
    - Segment NPS by cabin class, travel route, or booking platform
    - Close the loop fast especially for Detractors after delays, complaints, or escalations
    - Use Promoter testimonials in loyalty marketing and cross-sell campaigns

2. Social Cause & Community Service (e.g., Pilgrimage Support)

"Serving people's spirit is as much about dignity as it is about logistics."

- **What:** NPS here reflects emotional resonance and perceived care during deeply personal journeys.
- **Why:** Satisfaction is often unspoken; loyalty depends on dignity, empathy, and seamlessness.
- **How:** Use simplified, heartfelt NPS language:
- *"Would you recommend this service to another family/member/devotee?"*
- **When:** After the end of service or at key transition points (e.g., arrival, farewell).
- **Takeaways:**
    - Use storytelling and feedback loops to humanize volunteer training
    - Track improvements in trust and safety over time
    - Engage promoters as brand stewards or donors

3. Restaurants & F&B

"A great meal fades but a great experience brings people back."

- **What:** NPS captures overall impression beyond food, including service, ambiance, and ease.
- **Why:** Dining is sensory and social; one Detractor can post a harmful review, while a Promoter fills tables.
- **How:** Integrate NPS into e-bills, QR codes on menus, loyalty apps, or SMS follow-ups.
- **When:** Immediately after dining for peak recall, or within a few hours.
- **Takeaways:**
    - Map NPS by outlet, meal period, staff on shift
    - Address Detractors privately and swiftly
    - Highlight Promoter reviews in online visibility efforts

4. Coaching & Education Services

"When you teach well, your students promote you better than any ad."

- **What:** NPS reveals how deeply a student values the *experience of learning* not just grades.
- **Why:** Emotional and intellectual resonance determine repeat enrolments and referrals.
- **How:** Run surveys post-course, workshop, or term. Ask:
- *"How likely are you to recommend this program/faculty to your peers?"*
- **When:** At end of engagement, and optionally mid-way for real-time calibration.
- **Takeaways:**
    - Track variance by topic, mode (online/offline), and facilitator

- Use feedback to improve curriculum design and delivery
- Leverage Promoters as testimonials or alumni advocates

Snapshot: Cross-Industry Summary

Sector	NPS Value Lens	Touchpoint for Deployment	Special Tip
Travel & Airlines	Comfort, resolution, memory	24–48 hrs post-trip	Convert Promoters into loyalty members
Community Services	Dignity, service, empathy	At journey close	Use NPS stories to train volunteers
Restaurants	Sensory delight, pace	Immediately post-meal	Link scores to shift rosters or staff rewards
Coaching & Education	Transformation, clarity	Post-course or term-end	Map scores to instructor or format style

Optional Framework: Industry NPS Fit Matrix

Industry	Emotional Sensitivity	Volume of Interaction	Advocacy Influence	NPS Priority
Travel	Very High	Moderate–High	High	Top 2 KPI
Community Services	High	Moderate	High	Culture & Training
Restaurants	Moderate	High	Medium–High	Daily Pulse
Coaching	High	Low–Moderate	High	Loyalty Engine

Final Takeaway

While the *What* of NPS stays constant measuring loyalty, predicting growth, listening deeply the *How* must be shaped by the **soul of the sector**.

A hotel chain may build journeys. A coaching brand may build transformation. A social service may build healing. Regardless, NPS is your lens and your lever.

"In every sector, trust travels faster through people than through promotions. NPS lets you listen to trust, act on it, and earn it again."

Would you like me to create a visual graphic or diagnostic checklist to accompany this chapter for workshop use? I can also prepare sector-specific NPS scripts if you'd like to include them in your Tools appendix. Let's wrap this book with the same thoughtfulness and resonance it started with.

Industry NPS Readiness Diagnostic

"Are We Listening Right?"

For each industry below, rate yourself (1 = Not at all, 5 = Fully implemented):

Question	Travel	Community	Restaurant	Education
We have defined customer personas and expectations				
We collect NPS at the *right moment* post-experience				
Our NPS surveys use *language suited* to our audience				
Detractor comments are tracked and				

actioned by specific teams				
We identify Promoters and use their feedback in marketing/referrals				
NPS trends are reviewed monthly by cross-functional leaders				
We benchmark NPS over time or against peers in our sector				
Our staff are trained in empathy and closing the loop with customers				
NPS is linked to staff KPAs, incentives, or performance improvement				

Interpretation:

- 35–45: Sector-leading CX capability
- 25–34: Good practice some gaps to address
- Below 25: NPS is likely not yet driving meaningful change

Chapter 19:
Action Speaks Louder Than Words

From Learning Wow to Implementation Wow!

Chapter Objective

To help readers convert customer-centric learnings into execution building lasting change through planning, commitment, and rhythm across organizations of all sizes.

1. Why Most CX Learning Fizzles Out

Leaders attend workshops. Teams gather insights. Surveys reveal truths.

But then:

- Notes are archived
- Insights aren't assigned
- Change feels optional

This chapter is your **call to activation**. Because CX doesn't change lives until it changes your **calendar, cadence, and culture**.

"Learning without execution is inspiration without impact."

2. The Cost of Inaction

What happens when CX isn't acted upon?

- Detractor complaints escalate into churn
- Promoter goodwill decays through neglect
- Frontline teams disengage
- Customers stop speaking up

CX that isn't activated becomes **decoration**. The goal is to make it a **muscle**.

3. Planning CX Like a Business Strategy

You wouldn't run finance without forecasts. You wouldn't manage HR without KPAs.

So why should CX be instinctive or ad hoc?

CX Planning Essentials

Component	What It Ensures
CX Charter	Shared beliefs, promises, escalation paths
Experience Calendar	Fixed reviews, events, team rituals
CX KPAs	Role-linked metrics and accountabilities
Sprint Board	Actioned improvements tracked by theme

"If you fail to plan CX, you plan to disappoint customers."

4. Converting the Learning "Wow" Into Implementation "Wow"

Learning excites. Implementation sustains.

Flip Your Rituals

Learning Ritual	How to Convert into Execution Ritual
Insight Sharing	Monthly CX Retros with action plans
Workshop Takeaways	Sprint Tracker + Assigned Owners
NPS Score Celebration	Detractor Debrief → Quick Win Roadmap
Customer Testimonials	Frontline Recognition + Campaign Reuse
Complaint Logs	Root Cause Lab + Recovery Ritual Templates

Make reflection actionable. Make inspiration repeatable.

5. Organizational Momentum – For Any Size

Whether you're a solo entrepreneur or a multinational brand, CX begins **today**:

First Moves by Org Type

Organisation Type	Activation Action
Solo Entrepreneur	NPS follow-ups + gratitude messages
Small Business	CX dashboard → Staff training → Recovery Playbook
Mid-size Enterprise	Sprint Boards + CX Governance Council
Community Org	Empathy Training + Post-service Sentiment Logs

It is not about size. It's about sincerity.

6. Building Rhythms – Speed, Simplicity, Trust

Great CX cultures aren't louder. They're **faster**, **simpler**, and **more trusted**.

- **Speed** to resolve pain
- **Simplicity** in communication and process
- **Trust** through consistent follow-through

Don't chase trends. Build rituals.

First 90 Days CX Planner – Quick Reference

Timeline	Actions
Days 1–30	Audit journeys, CX metrics, customer verbatims
Days 31–60	Draft CX Charter, launch NPS cycles, assign sprint owners
Days 61–90	Embed CX reviews into meetings, launch empathy training, track impact

Final Takeaway

You've read frameworks. Studied empathy. Explored NPS.

Now, ask:

- What will be different in the next 90 days?
- Who owns each improvement?
- How will the customer notice?

Because the only experience that matters is the one that actually **happens**.

"Customers reward consistency. Teams respond to clarity. Brands grow through courage."

Make CX your habit not your highlight.

Chapter 20: The CX Leader's Mindset

"Building on our exploration of emotional intelligence in Chapter 4, where we saw how frontline empathy transforms customer interactions, this chapter shifts our focus to the leaders who architect and embody that empathy. Here, we'll expand from individual EQ skills to the triad of Architect, Empath, and Challenger archetypes showing how mindsets, not just metrics, drive lasting CX culture."

20.1 Introduction

In a customer-centric organization, leadership isn't a title, it's a way of thinking. This chapter explores how leaders shape culture through behaviour, emotional intelligence, and systems thinking. You'll discover why mindsets matter more than frameworks and how small shifts at the top cascade into organization-wide transformation.

20.2 What Makes a CX Mindset

A CX leader's mindset blends strategic clarity with human empathy. It's grounded in four core beliefs: customers are co-creators of value, feedback is a gift rather than a critique, frontline insights drive strategy, and trust is both metric and mandate. Embracing these beliefs moves leaders beyond process champion to culture architect.

20.3 Leadership Archetypes in CX

Every CX transformation needs diverse leadership roles. Three archetypes stand out:

- The Architect
  - Designs systems and rituals that embed customer focus into daily routines
  - Translates vision into scalable, measurable processes

- The Empath
    - Models active listening, emotional regulation, and vulnerability
    - Brings frontline stories into boardrooms to humanize data
- The Challenger
    - Questions inherited assumptions and outmoded KPIs
    - Sparks constructive tension to push teams toward breakthrough ideas

Effective CX leaders fluidly inhabit all three archetypes, adapting to context and culture.

20.4 Emotional Intelligence as a CX Competency

Emotional intelligence (EQ) underpins every customer interaction, yet it's too often sidelined in leadership development. A high-EQ CX leader:

- Self-regulates under stress to manage customer crises calmly
- Demonstrates social awareness by reading frontline teams' unspoken signals
- Uses empathy to translate customer emotions into design imperatives

By treating EQ as a core leadership skill, organizations cultivate deeper, more authentic customer connections.

20.5 Four Pillars of the CX Leader's Mindset

This model represents the mindset shift from transactional to transformational leadership:

Awareness

↑

Empathy → ← Agency

↓

Alignment

- Awareness: Constantly scans for customer signals VoC, market shifts, and frontline chatter.
- Empathy: Feels the customer's journey; elevates personal stories over raw metrics.
- Agency: Grants teams the freedom and resources to resolve issues, innovate, and experiment.
- Alignment: Ensures every function product, ops, finance pulls in the same customer-centric direction.

Together, these pillars enable leaders to make decisions that balance speed, scale, and sincerity.

20.6 Cultivating the Mindset: Practical Exercises

1. Daily CX Reflection
    - Block 5 minutes each morning to review a customer story or VOC excerpt.
    - Note one insight and one action you can take that day.
2. Gemba Walk with a Twist
    - Participate without agenda; listen more than speak.
    - Capture three frontline frustrations and propose a rapid-pilot solution.
3. Empathy Swap
    - Pair a leader with a frontline teammate for a full shift.
    - Debrief on emotional highs and lows; identify systemic blockers.
4. Leadership Book Club
    - Rotate CX-themed reads (e.g., *The Culture Code*, *Empathy-Driven Leadership*).

- Discuss real-world applications and revise team rituals accordingly.

20.7 Case Example: Vodafone India's Field Empowerment

At Vodafone India, senior leaders joined field teams for Gemba visits. Instead of auditing, they listened, tracking customer frustrations in rural markets and co-designing solutions on the spot. One leader discovered that a simple SIM-activation tweak could halve wait times. By empowering agents to implement it immediately, NPS rose significantly. This exemplifies how a CX mindset turns daily observations into rapid, customer-driven innovation.

20.8 Reflection & Action Questions

1. Which archetype (Architect, Empath, Challenger) feels most natural to you and least natural?
2. How often do you practice emotional regulation under customer pressure? What's your personal EQ plan?
3. Rate your organization on the Four Pillars model. Which pillar needs urgent attention?
4. What frontline ritual can you adopt this week to deepen your customer awareness?

20.9 Summary

A CX leader's mindset is the catalyst that moves customer-centricity from policy to practice. By embracing the Architect, Empath, and Challenger roles, honing emotional intelligence, and living the four pillars Awareness, Empathy, Agency, Alignment you'll ignite lasting change. In adopting this mindset, you don't just manage CX metrics you, transform them into meaningful narratives that guide your organization forward.

Chapter 21:
From Score to Story

"In Chapter 17, we introduced Net Promoter Score as a diagnostic tool for CX health. Now, in this chapter, we go one level deeper transforming those raw NPS and CSAT figures into compelling narratives that mobilize teams. You'll learn the four elements of storytelling and the storyboard tool first outlined in Chapter 9, linking metrics to meaning."

21.1 Introduction

Customer metrics are valuable but numbers alone rarely ignite change. In this chapter, we shift from viewing NPS, CSAT, and VOC as static scores to treating them as living narratives. You'll learn how to weave feedback into stories that inspire action, solidify culture, and guide strategy.

21.2 The Evolution of NPS: From Number to Narrative

- Early NPS practice treated scores as targets to hit and charts to monitor.
- The next frontier is releasing the story behind each score transforming raw data into emotional triggers that mobilize teams.
- When every datum carries a customer voice, your organization moves from reporting to relating.

21.3 Four Elements of CX Storytelling

To craft stories that resonate and drive accountability, each narrative needs:

1. Context
    - Who is the customer? What prompted their feedback?

2. Conflict
    - What pain point or frustration did they experience?
3. Resolution
    - How did your team respond or how could they have responded?
4. Impact
    - What changed for the customer, the team, or the business as a result?

When you structure customer anecdotes this way, stories become repeatable templates for problem solving and celebration.

21.4 Integrating Metrics and Story: The Feedback Loop

1. Collect – Capture both the quantitative score and the verbatim comment.
2. Curate – Identify stories that illustrate systemic issues or breakthrough moments.
3. Communicate – Share the chosen narratives in huddles, newsletters, and leadership briefs.
4. Act – Assign clear owners to follow up on each story, with defined timelines and outcomes.
5. Close the Loop – Report back to the customer and the organization on actions taken, completing the cycle of transparency and trust.

21.5 The Storyboard Tool

A simple visual aid to map metrics to narratives:

Score Range	Customer Quote	Story Element	Action Owner	Status
0–6	"My install took three visits."	Conflict	Field Ops Manager	In Progress
7–8	"Rep was polite but scripted."	Context & Conflict	CX Trainer	Completed
9–10	"Upgraded my plan free of charge wow!"	Resolution & Impact	Service Lead	Celebrated

Use this storyboard in weekly CX forums to keep metrics human and momentum high.

21.6 Case Example: Turning a Detractor into a Movement

At a healthcare provider, an NPS survey flagged a detractor: "Long wait times. Felt unheard."

- Context: First-time patient at a high-volume clinic.
- Conflict: Reception understaffed; patient passed through without empathy.
- Resolution: Clinic manager shadowed the front desk for a week, reorganized shift schedules, and introduced a "first five minutes" greeting protocol.
- Impact: Wait-time complaints halved in two months; staff morale soared.

The story was featured in the company newsletter and became the catalyst for a cross-functional "Empathy in Admissions" workshop, embedding narrative-driven improvement into daily routines.

21.7 Practical Exercises

1. Story Mining Session
   - Gather 5 recent NPS detractor comments.
   - In small groups, apply the Four Elements and draft full narratives.
2. CX Story Jam
   - Invite frontline teams to share one "WOW" story and one "Woe" story.
   - Vote on the most instructive narratives and plan "next-step" experiments.
3. Boardroom Brief
   - Present a two-minute story instead of a chart in your next leadership meeting.
   - Observe the difference in engagement and follow-up actions.

21.8 Reflection & Action Questions

1. Which recent customer story moved you more deeply: a promoter's praise or a detractor's frustration and why?
2. How can you adjust your next NPS review to spotlight one compelling narrative over raw numbers?
3. What rituals can you introduce to surface hidden stories in your team beyond the monthly report?
4. Who will you invite to co-craft your first CX storyboard, ensuring cross-functional buy-in?

21.9 Summary

When metrics become stories, they transcend spreadsheets and energize people. By structuring feedback into context, conflict, resolution, and impact and by using tools like the CX storyboard you turn cold data into catalytic narratives. In doing so, you elevate NPS from a reporting requirement to a movement-building force. The next chapter will explore how to operationalize trust at every level, ensuring your stories aren't just heard they're heeded.

Chapter 22:
Designing for Trust

"Trust first surfaced in Chapter 5 as a critical CX dimension alongside competence and reliability. This chapter picks up that thread with a hands-on Trust Audit framework, turning conceptual pillars into concrete diagnostics and system-level redesigns that embed integrity and benevolence into every touchpoint."

22.1 Introduction

Trust is the invisible infrastructure of any customer-centric organization. When customers believe you will deliver consistently, they engage more, advocate more, and forgive more. This chapter equips you with a systematic approach to audit, design, and embed trust across your processes, policies, and people.

22.2 Why Trust Matters in CX

- Trust reduces friction: customers move faster through journeys when they believe you'll "do the right thing."
- Trust drives advocacy: satisfied customers become vocal champions when they feel safe and respected.
- Trust underpins resilience: in crisis moments, organizations with strong trust capital recover more quickly.

22.3 The Four Dimensions of Trust

Designing for trust begins by understanding its pillars:

Dimension	Definition	CX Implication
Competence	Delivering on promises with expertise and consistency	Accurate billing, timely fulfilment, knowledgeable reps
Reliability	Maintaining dependable performance over time	Zero-surprise policies, predictable support SLAs
Integrity	Acting with honesty, transparency, and ethical intent	Clear T&Cs, proactive communication on issues
Benevolence	Demonstrating genuine care for customer wellbeing	Personalized outreach, empathy in complaint handling

A holistic trust design addresses each dimension not just competence.

22.4 The Trust Audit Framework

Use this four-step tool to diagnose and shore up trust gaps:

1. Map Touchpoints
    - List all customer interactions (sales, service, billing, digital).
2. Evaluate Against Dimensions
    - Rate each touchpoint 1–5 on competence, reliability, integrity, benevolence.
3. Identify Low-Trust Zones
    - Highlight interactions scoring 3 or below in any dimension.

4. Design Remediations
    - For each low-trust zone, define process tweaks, training needs, or policy changes.

22.5 Embedding Trust into Systems

1. Policy Transparency
    - Publish plain-language T&Cs and FAQs; remove hidden fees.
2. Process Simplicity
    - Streamline common requests (returns, upgrades) to require fewer steps.
3. Empowered Frontline
    - Give reps authority to resolve issues up to a defined financial threshold without escalation.
4. Governance Rituals
    - Weekly "Trust Huddle" to review flagged interactions; assign owners for follow-up.

22.6 Case Example: A telecom company's Trust Sprint

When a telecom company launched a new prepaid data plan, initial complaints centred on confusing activation steps. Applying the Trust Audit:

- Touchpoint: USSD activation (Reliability score: 2)
- Remediation: Redesigned USSD flow to two simple prompts and added a confirmation SMS.
- Outcome: 40% drop in activation-related detractor comments and a 5-point uptick in regional NPS within four weeks.

22.7 Practical Exercises

1. Touchpoint Trust Mapping

- In cross-functional pairs, list 10 key customer touchpoints and rate them on the four trust dimensions.
- Identify the top two "trust blockers" to tackle immediately.

2. Policy Plain-Speak Workshop
   - Rewrite one complex policy or T&C passage in everyday language.
   - Test with a small customer focus group for clarity and tone.
3. Empowerment Role-Play
   - Simulate a call where the rep must decide on a goodwill gesture.
   - Debrief: How did access to authority affect empathy, speed, and resolution?

22.8 Reflection & Action Questions

1. Which trust dimension is your organization strongest in and which needs urgent focus?
2. How does your current governance cadence surface low-trust incidents?
3. What single process simplification could immediately boost reliability?
4. Who in your leadership team needs a "Trust Walk" visiting customers and frontline teams to hear unfiltered feedback?

22.9 Summary

Designing for trust is not a one-off project, it's a mindset and a system. By auditing touchpoints, embedding transparency, and empowering teams, you transform trust from aspiration into infrastructure. With trust firmly in place, every customer interaction becomes a hand-off of confidence, driving loyalty and advocacy that endure.

Chapter 23:
Future-Fit Organizations

"In Chapter 8 we mapped the CX maturity pathway from Foundational to Strategic. Here, we extend that model into an "Anticipatory" stage and introduce five future-fit attributes agility, ecosystem thinking, digital-human convergence, continuous learning, and purpose alignment so you can chart a roadmap from today's state to tomorrow's innovations."

23.1 Introduction

The pace of change in markets, technology, and customer expectations demands organizations that can sense shifts, adapt swiftly, and innovate continuously. In this chapter, you'll discover what it means to be future-fit not just resilient, but proactive in shaping tomorrow's customer experience. We'll explore the attributes, maturity pathway, and a deep-dive case study that illustrates how to transform your organization into a CX-driven, future-ready powerhouse.

23.2 Defining Future-Fit

A future-fit organization:

- Anticipates customer needs before they surface
- Breaks down silos to enable seamless, cross-functional collaboration
- Infuses digital and human channels with equal agility
- Cultivates a learning culture that embraces experimentation and failure
- Aligns its purpose, strategy, and metrics around continuous customer-centric evolution

Becoming future-fit means evolving from "we'll fix it later" to "we're building tomorrow's solutions today."

23.3 Five Attributes of Future-Fit Organizations

Attribute	Description
1. Agile Operating Model	Small, empowered teams run rapid pilots iterating on customer feedback in days, not months.
2. Customer-Led Ecosystem	Partners, suppliers, and internal functions unite around shared CX goals and transparent data flows.
3. Digital-Human Convergence	Seamless journeys where bots handle routine tasks and humans resolve exceptions with empathy.
4. Continuous Learning Culture	Regular "fail fast" rituals, knowledge-sharing huddles, and open post-mortems normalize growth.
5. Purpose-Driven Alignment	A north-star vision (beyond profit) galvanizes teams to prioritize customer and community impact.

These attributes are interdependent; agility falters without shared purpose, and digital investments stall without continuous learning.

23.4 The CX Maturity Pathway

Organizations advance through four CX maturity stages on their future-fit journey:

1. Foundational

   – CX awareness is nascent; metrics are siloed.

2. Operational

   – Processes exist but lack cross-functional integration.

3. Strategic

   – Customer insights inform roadmaps; leadership sponsorship is active.

4. Anticipatory

   – Predictive analytics, co-creation with customers, and ecosystem orchestration drive innovation.

Use this model to benchmark your current state and plot a roadmap to Anticipatory CX.

23.5 Detailed Case Study: Royal Hospitals' Patient-Centric Evolution

23.5.1 Background & Challenges

Royal Hospitals, a leading healthcare network in India, faced mounting patient dissatisfaction in its outpatient services. Key pain points included:

- Average wait times exceeding 90 minutes
- Fragmented communication between reception, clinicians, and billing
- Lack of real-time visibility on appointment status
- Low staff morale due to repeated patient complaints

These issues eroded trust, drove down NPS scores, and risked brand reputation in a highly competitive market.

23.5.2 Interventions & Implementation

Royal launched a "Patient First Sprint" a rapid, cross-functional initiative designed to diagnose and resolve root causes within six weeks.

1. Cross-Functional Sprint Team

   - Roles: Operations manager, IT lead, clinical coordinator, patient liaison, data analyst

- Empowerment: Authority to prototype process changes without lengthy approvals

2. Touchpoint Mapping & Prioritization
    - Mapped 15 critical outpatient touchpoints from digital booking to post-visit feedback
    - Rated each on the four trust dimensions (Competence, Reliability, Integrity, Benevolence)
    - Identified top three "trust blockers" (e.g., queue management, information handoffs)
3. Rapid Prototyping
    - Digital Queue Dashboard: Mobile interface showing real-time slot updates and expected wait times
    - "First Five Minutes" Protocol: Receptionists greeted patients by name, outlined next steps, and provided approximate wait durations
    - Learning Labs: Weekly 90-minute forums where frontline staff shared patient stories and co-designed small experiments
4. Feedback Loops
    - Post-visit SMS surveys (CSAT + open comments) delivered within two hours of discharge
    - Weekly sprint-team review of survey verbatims to refine interventions on the fly

23.5.3 Outcomes & Impact

Metric	Before Sprint	After Sprint	Change
Average Wait Time	92 minutes	64 minutes	–30%
Outpatient NPS	48	60	+12 points
Patient Complaints on Queueing	42 per week	16 per week	–62%
Staff-reported Morale (Internal EQ)	3.2/5	4.1/5	+0.9 points
Adoption of "First Five Minutes"	0%	85% of shifts	Rapid cultural uptake

These results not only boosted patient satisfaction and trust but also built a repeatable sprint model now rolling out to other service lines.

23.5.4 Reflection Questions

1. How would you structure a cross-functional sprint team in your own organization?
2. Which customer touchpoints would you map first, and why?
3. What rapid-prototype interventions could you pilot to reduce customer friction?
4. How would you design feedback loops to ensure continuous improvement?

23.5.5 Discussion & Probable Solutions

1. Sprint Team Structure
    - Include operations, technology, frontline service, and a customer advocate.
    - Empower the team with clear mandate, budget cap, and decision-making authority for quick turnarounds.
2. Touchpoint Prioritization

- Begin with high-impact, high-visibility interactions (e.g., first greeting, payment).
- Use simple ratings against trust dimensions to pinpoint bottlenecks.

3. Rapid-Prototype Ideas
    - Digital signage or mobile alerts for queue status.
    - Staff "welcome scripts" that set expectations and show empathy.
    - Low-cost amenities (water stations, charging points) to improve perceived wait times.
4. Designing Feedback Loops
    - Short CSAT surveys via SMS or email within hours of service.
    - Weekly "Storyboard Sessions" where the sprint team reviews verbatim comments, selects one "WOW" and one "Woe" story, and assigns rapid follow-up actions.
    - Monthly leadership briefs highlighting key lessons and celebrating small wins.

23.6 Practical Exercises

1. Future-Fit Self-Assessment
    - Rate your organization on the five attributes (Section 23.3). Identify one high-impact action for each.
2. Cross-Functional Sprint Simulation
    - Assemble a mock sprint team (operations, IT, marketing, service).
    - Assign a customer pain point and run a two-hour ideation and prototype session.

3. Learning Lab Design
    - Plan a recurring forum where frontline teams and leaders share customer stories, experiment results, and "what-next" plans.

23.7 Reflection & Action Questions

1. Which CX maturity stage best describes your organization today and what will it take to reach the next?
2. How might you pilot a "Patient First Sprint" or equivalent in your context?
3. What one attribute of a future-fit organization can you champion immediately?
4. Who are your ecosystem partners, and how could you deepen collaboration around CX outcomes?

23.8 Summary

Future-fit organizations don't wait for disruption they drive it by embedding agility, ecosystem thinking, digital-human convergence, continuous learning, and purpose into every fibre of their culture. By assessing your current CX maturity, running rapid sprints, and institutionalizing Learning Labs, you'll not only meet tomorrow's customer expectations you'll shape them. The movement is in your hands.

Chapter 24:
The Movement Begins

"Our deep dive on rituals in Chapter 6 showed how simple habits reinforce CX values. Now, we scale those rituals into a movement by identifying and empowering a network of CX champions, formalizing governance from Chapter 12's leadership frameworks, and embedding rituals into performance systems for sustainable impact."

24.0 Chapter Objectives

- Identify, recruit, and empower a network of CX champions across your organization
- Design and embed rituals that sustain momentum and shape culture
- Build governance structures that institutionalize the movement
- Measure and scale your CX movement for enduring impact

24.1 Introduction

Customer-centric transformation doesn't end when processes improve, it thrives when a movement takes hold. In this chapter, you transition from implementing frameworks to mobilizing people. You'll learn how to seed, nourish, and govern a CX movement that outlives any single project or leader.

24.2 Identifying and Empowering CX Champions

24.2.1 Mapping the Network

- Conduct a Stakeholder Influence Audit:
    1. List all functions touching customers (service, product, marketing, HR, finance)

2. Rate individuals on passion, influence, and openness to change (scale 1–5)
3. Spotlight connectors, those who bridge silos, and potential evangelists

24.2.2 Role Definitions

- Connector: Builds cross-team bridges, shares insights, and surfaces needs
- Storyteller: Crafts and shares customer narratives to inspire action
- Analyzer: Digs into data, links feedback to business outcomes
- Evangelist: Publicly celebrates wins, recruits new champions

24.2.3 Empowerment Playbook

- Issue a "Champion Charter": Defines purpose, decision rights, and a small discretionary budget
- Provide Toolkits: Storyboard templates, trust-audit checklists, sprint blueprints
- Schedule Onboarding Workshops: Deep-dive into CX principles, rituals, and reporting cadence

24.3 Rituals and Tools for Sustaining Momentum

24.3.1 Weekly CX Story Jam

- Format: 30 minutes, remote or in-person
- Agenda: One "WOW" story + one "Woe" story → rapid 5-minute experiment plan
- Toolkit: Storyboard worksheet, action tracker

24.3.2 Monthly Trust Huddle

- Purpose: Surface low-trust touchpoints using the Trust Audit Framework (Ch. 22)

- Participants: Champions, process owners, one executive sponsor
- Outcome: Prioritized remediations, owner assignments, and timeline

24.3.3 Quarterly Movement Summit

- Showcase: Sprint results, customer stories, unexpected learnings
- Format: Lightning talks, panels, mini-hackathons
- Sponsors: C-suite guests, external CX thought leaders

24.3.4 Digital Movement Hub

- Platform: Intranet portal or dedicated channel in collaboration tools
- Features:
    - Champion directory and contact links
    - Repository of case studies, toolkits, and recorded sessions
    - Live feedback board for cross-pollination of ideas

24.4 Governance and Scaling

24.4.1 Embedding into Performance Management

- Tie Champion KPIs to performance reviews and variable compensation
- Include CX metrics (e.g., local NPS improvements, number of experiments run)

24.4.2 CX Steering Committee

- Composition: C-suite sponsor, Head of CX, champion representatives
- Cadence: Bi-monthly, with a rotating champion as co-chair

- Charter:
    - Remove blockers and channel resources
    - Validate new rituals and scale successful pilots
    - Review movement health dashboard

24.4.3 Budgeting for Experimentation

- Allocate a line item for "CX Movement Fund" to cover small-scale pilots, design sprints, and learning labs
- Define spending thresholds for champions to act autonomously

24.4.4 Communities of Practice

- Pair seasoned champions with newcomers in mentorship pods
- Host quarterly "Champion Exchanges" to share playbooks and deepen expertise

24.5 Case Study Deep Dive: Champion Network at Vodafone India

24.5.1 Situation

Vodafone India aimed to boost NPS in semi-urban regions but lacked localized ownership of CX initiatives.

24.5.2 Approach

1. Champion Selection: Identified 12 regional agents, marketing leads, and tech champions based on influence scores.
2. Charter Workshop: Co-created roles, rituals, and success metrics in a two-day offsite.
3. Ritual Launch: Rolled out Weekly Story Jams and Quarterly Summits virtually across 15 locations.
4. Governance Link: Embedded champions into the existing Quality Steering Committee with a dedicated "CX Flash" segment.

24.5.3 Impact

Metric	Before	After	Change
Regional NPS (average)	42	53	+11 points
Champion-led Experiments	0	28 in 6 months	Movement scaled
Cross-Functional Projects	2 per quarter	7 per quarter	+250%
Feeling of Agency (surveyed)	2.8/5	4.2/5	+1.4 points

24.5.4 Discussion Questions

1. How did Vodafone balance top-down sponsorship with bottom-up autonomy?
2. Which ritual had the greatest impact on champion engagement and why?
3. What governance link ensured the movement was not siloed?
4. How might you adapt this champion model to your organization's size and structure?

24.6 Advanced Exercises

1. Champion Incubator Workshop (Half-day)
   - Draft network maps, role charters, and pilot ideation for your first cohort.
2. Ritual Design Sprint (Two hours)
   - Break into teams to prototype one new CX ritual pitch ceremonies, empathy lunches, surprise audits.
3. Governance Simulation (90 minutes)
   - Role-play a CX steering committee meeting to unblock a stalled pilot and allocate resources.

24.7 Reflection & Action Questions

1. Which five individuals will you invite as your inaugural CX champions and what criteria guided your choices?
2. What new ritual will you prototype this month, and which metrics will you track for its success?
3. How will you integrate the CX movement fund into your budgeting cycle?
4. What success stories will you celebrate at your first Quarterly Movement Summit?

24.8 Summary

Building a CX movement means shifting from projects to people, from one-off wins to lasting rituals, and from departmental programs to institutional governance. By mapping and empowering champions, embedding sustaining rituals, and formalizing governance, you create a living, breathing movement one that carries the spirit of *Beyond Satisfaction* forward and sets the stage for your next evolution in customer-centric leadership. The movement truly begins now.

Chapter 25:
Co-Creating a Customer-Centric Ecosystem

"Chapter 4 illuminated the power of cross-functional collaboration within your own organization. In this final chapter, we widen the lens beyond your walls mapping external partners, building customer communities, and leveraging technology platforms so your CX movement radiates outward, uniting suppliers, regulators, and advocates in shared value creation."

25.1 Introduction

Customer-centricity doesn't stop at your organization's doors it radiates outward through partners, communities, and platforms. In this chapter, you'll learn how to forge an ecosystem that amplifies your CX movement, turning isolated wins into collective impact. We'll cover ecosystem mapping, community building, technology enablers, movement health metrics, and a deep-dive case study.

25.2 Ecosystem Partnerships

Building an ecosystem starts with identifying and aligning with external stakeholders who share your CX vision.

- Partner Mapping
    1. List all external entities that touch your customer journey (suppliers, distributors, agencies, tech vendors, regulators).
    2. Rate each on strategic fit, customer impact potential, and collaboration readiness (scale 1–5).
    3. Select 2–3 high-leverage partners for co-innovation pilots.

- Joint Value Propositions
    - Co-develop offerings that solve customer pain points end-to-end.
    - Define shared success metrics (e.g., combined NPS uplift, cross-sell rates).
- Governance & Data-Sharing
    - Establish a bi-monthly "Ecosystem Council" with clear data-governance rules.
    - Use secure APIs or portals for real-time insight exchange.

25.3 Building Customer Communities

A thriving community turns customers into advocates and co-creators.

- Online Hubs & Forums
    - Launch branded communities (e.g., Slack, proprietary platforms) for product feedback, peer support, and idea crowdsourcing.
    - Seed early discussions with exclusive content and expert Q&A sessions.
- In-Person Events & Workshops
    - Host local meetups, customer councils, or user conferences to deepen engagement.
    - Rotate themes "Innovation Day," "Empathy Lab," "Voice of Customer Jam."
- Ambassador Programs
    - Recruit super-users as community moderators and beta testers.
    - Reward contributions with early access, swag, or public recognition.

25.4 Technology as an Enabler

The right platforms and tools accelerate ecosystem coordination and community vibrancy.

Capability	Example Tools	Purpose
Community Platforms	Discourse, Tribe, Slack	Host discussions, track sentiment, spotlight top contributors
Experience Portals	Salesforce Community Cloud, Zendesk	Integrate support, knowledge base, and customer feedback feeds
Analytics & Dashboards	Tableau, Power BI, Looker	Visualize joint KPIs, ecosystem health, and engagement trends
Workflow Automations	Zapier, Workato, Microsoft Power Automate	Streamline partner handoffs and community notifications

25.5 Measuring Movement Health

Beyond internal metrics, track these ecosystem indicators:

- Network Growth: Number of active partners, community members, and ambassadors.
- Engagement Depth: Forum posts, event attendance, co-creation submissions.
- Shared Outcomes: Joint NPS uplift, referral volume, cross-sell revenue.
- Collaboration Velocity: Time from pilot proposal to live deployment.

Use a quarterly "Ecosystem Health Dashboard" to keep leadership and partners aligned.

25.6 Detailed Case Study: Airbnb's Host & Guest Community

25.6.1 Background & Challenge

Airbnb needed to scale trust rapidly between millions of guests and hosts across geographies, ensuring consistent experiences without centralized control.

25.6.2 Interventions & Implementation

1. Host Community Hubs
   - Launched online forums and regional Meetups to share best practices.
2. Host Guarantee & Support
   - Introduced a host protection insurance and 24/7 support line to bolster confidence.
3. Co-Creation Labs
   - Invited top hosts to prototype new features (e.g., Smart Pricing, Experiences).
4. Technology Integration
   - Built a host dashboard with sentiment analytics, local event calendars, and training modules.

25.6.3 Outcomes & Impact

Metric	Before	After	Change
Active Host Participation	15% of hosts	45% of hosts	+200%
Host Retention Rate	60% annual	80% annual	+20 points
Community Forum Monthly Posts	8,000	25,000	+212%
Co-Created Product Features Launched	0	6 in one year	New innovation stream

25.6.4 Reflection Questions

1. What criteria would you use to select partners or customers for a co-creation lab?
2. How can you replicate Airbnb's trust guarantees in your own ecosystem?
3. Which technology enabler would yield the fastest engagement lift?
4. How will you surface community-driven insights back into product or service roadmaps?

25.7 Practical Exercises

1. Ecosystem Blueprint
    - Draft a visual map of key partners, customers, and platforms in your ecosystem.
    - Identify 3 "white-space" collaboration opportunities.
2. Community Kickstart Plan
    - Outline the first 3 months of online and offline community activities, including themes, channels, and incentives.
3. Tech Stack Lite
    - Choose one analytics and one engagement tool; plan a proof-of-value pilot with clear success criteria.

25.8 Summary

Scaling your CX movement into an ecosystem unleashes exponential value. By strategically partnering, nurturing communities, leveraging technology, and tracking movement health, you transform isolated wins into collective momentum. Airbnb's journey reminds us that when hosts, guests, and platform co-create trust, innovation and loyalty flourish. Your ecosystem awaits, co-create it thoughtfully, measure it diligently, and watch your movement ripple outward.

Epilogue

NPS: A Lens, A Lever, A Legacy

Customer centricity has no finish line, only deeper clarity.

Whether you run a restaurant or an airline, a classroom or a call centre, the heartbeat of loyalty is not efficiency, but **empathy**. NPS doesn't just ask "Were they happy?" - it asks, *"Would they carry your story forward?"*

And that's the real test of value.

In the chapters ahead, you've seen frameworks, scripts, and metrics. But between every number lies a person. Between every "10" is a moment that mattered. And behind every "0" is a voice that wanted to be heard.

So, listen. Act. Adapt.

Earn their trust not once, but over and over again.

"The most powerful metric isn't what's measured. It's what moves people to remember you."

Beyond Satisfaction – Activation Toolkit

Appendix A – Glossary of CX Terms and Frameworks

Quick-reference definitions and models used throughout the book.

- **CX Metrics**: NPS, CSAT, CES, VoC
- **Customer Experience Models**: EMPACT (Empathy), Recovery NPS, CLV
- **Operational Concepts**: CX Charter, Sprints, Experience Labs
- **Lean Principles**: Muda (Waste), Mura (Variation), Muri (Burden)
- **Loyalty Types**: Emotional vs Transactional

Appendix B – Centricity Playbook Toolkit

Templates and trackers to embed CX into daily practice.

Tool	Use Case	Chapter Ref.
CX Maturity Diagnostic	Assess centricity depth across 5 levels	Ch. 17
Journey Mapping Canvas	Capture touchpoints, emotions, ownership	Ch. 8
CX KPA Tracker	Define KPAs across business functions	Ch. 10
Sprint Planning Template	Manage 2–3-week CX improvement cycles	Ch. 9
Sprint Progress Ledger	Record actions, results, follow-ups	Ch. 13
CX Ritual Calendar	Schedule reviews, huddles, retrospectives	Ch. 19

Appendix C – Complaint Wisdom System Tools

Turn customer complaints into recovery and reform assets.

- **Complaint Categorization Matrix** → Tag type, tone, urgency
- **Recovery Ritual Templates** → Train teams on empathy-based response
- **Root Cause Mapper** → Connect NPS feedback to systemic gaps
- **Playback Library Guide** → Build emotional case studies for training
- **"Voice of Disappointment" Lab Format** → Debrief unresolved pain points
- **Reference**: Chapter 14

Appendix D – Sectoral NPS Readiness Toolkit

Adapting NPS engagement across industries.

Element	Industries	Chapter Ref.
NPS Diagnostic Checklist	Travel, F&B, Education	Ch. 18
Sector-Specific Survey Scripts	Hospitality, Community	Ch. 18
Fit Matrix (Emotion vs Advocacy)	All sectors	Ch. 18
Deployment Timing Recommendations	High-touch experiences	Ch. 18

Appendix E – Execution Accelerator: First 90 Days Planner

Your roadmap for CX rollout and rhythm.

Phase	Sample Actions	Chapter Ref.
Days 1–30	Audit journeys, review CX data, identify quick wins	Ch. 19
Days 31–60	Launch NPS cycles, draft CX Charter, onboard CX stewards	Ch. 19
Days 61–90	Schedule retrospectives, train teams, embed CX KPAs	Ch. 19

Includes:

✓ Role Ownership Map

✓ Sprint Kick off Checklist

✓ Council Review Agenda Template

About the Author

Dr. Saifuddin Kapasi is an accomplished business leader, educator, and strategic advisor with over three decades of experience. After 17 transformative years at Vodafone India Ltd, he now leads as Promoter Director of Inflection Point and Business Head at Vaux Bicycle Industries.

A passionate advocate of human-centered performance and customer-centric excellence, Dr. Kapasi blends deep corporate insight with academic rigor. He serves as Visiting Faculty at Sydenham Institute of Management Studies Research and Entrepreneurship Education and Burhani College, where he mentors future leaders in programs such as MMS, MFM, MMM, BMS, and BAMMC.

Across boardrooms and classrooms, his philosophy is grounded in clarity, fairness, and impact. This book is a culmination of his enduring commitment to aligning strategy with execution and customers with the heart of every decision.

Final Note - Why the Journey Matters

Dear Reader,

I haven't written this book to showcase expertise, I've written it to spark action, empathy, and courage.

If you've reached this final page, thank you. Not just for reading, but for believing that customer centricity can be more than a strategy, it can be a mindset. A movement. A measure of who we truly are when we serve.

This book is for the quiet reformers. The CX champions behind the scenes. The leaders who listen when it's inconvenient. The teams who dare to ask, *"How did this make the customer feel?"*

I've spent decades exploring what makes loyalty last, what turns complaints into change, and what brings dignity into data. But what matters most is what **you** choose to do next.

Because when you lead with empathy…

When you close the loop with care…

When you celebrate the voice of your customer, not just the metrics…

That's when centricity becomes culture.

That's when the journey matters.

Customer trust at heart,

Dr. Saifuddin Kapasi

Primary Genre: Business & Management / Customer Experience (CX)

Positioning Statement:

A strategic and human-Centered guide for aspirational professionals in customer service and collaborative cross-functional teams seeking to elevate trust, empathy, and excellence in organizational culture.